PARENTING
AN ATHLETE

ANNETTE REITER

PARENTING
AN ATHLETE

TATE PUBLISHING & Enterprises

Parenting an Athlete
Copyright © 2011 by Annete Reiter. All rights reserved.

This book is designed to provide accurate and authoritative information with regard to the subject matter covered. This information is given with the understanding that neither the author nor Tate Publishing, LLC is engaged in rendering legal, professional advice. Since the details of your situation are fact dependent, you should additionally seek the services of a competent professional.

The opinions expressed by the author are not necessarily those of Tate Publishing, LLC.

Published by Tate Publishing & Enterprises, LLC
127 E. Trade Center Terrace | Mustang, Oklahoma 73064 USA
1.888.361.9473 | www.tatepublishing.com

Tate Publishing is committed to excellence in the publishing industry. The company reflects the philosophy established by the founders, based on Psalm 68:11,
"The Lord gave the word and great was the company of those who published it."

Book design copyright © 2011 by Tate Publishing, LLC. All rights reserved.
Cover design by Kenna Davis
Interior design by Stephanie Woloszyn

Published in the United States of America

ISBN: 978-1-61777-401-0
1. Sports & Recreation / Sports Psychology
2. Family & Relationships / Parenting / General
11.04.15

DEDICATION

To my dad and mom, Michael Angelotti and Marilyn Angelotti Kelly, who taught me so much about life through sports. My dad, Michael, was only in my life for nineteen short years, was a man of integrity and character, and taught me through example, accountability, and perseverance. My mom, Marilyn, is truly the best person I have ever known and taught me and continues to teach me respect for one's self and for others. Through her daily example she exemplifies unconditional love and kindness to others, selflessness, humility, and the true meaning of family. God sincerely blessed me.

To my husband and best friend, Dave, the absolute love of my life.

To my children, Brad, Alyssa, and Kristina, my pride for you is immeasurable. You are my heart.

ACKNOWLEDGMENTS

To my family who continues to support me in all my coaching endeavors and in every aspect of life. To my sister, Lisa, who first gave me the love and passion to coach. To my stepdad, Dick Kelly, who encouraged me to share my experiences and write this book.

A sincere thank you to the coaches and parents who were interviewed and shared their experiences: Dennis Murphy, Linda Murphy, Brad Ward, Karyn Pickard, Julie McHenry, and Jerry Campbell. And to Dr. Jim Karustis for his professional insight. Thanks also to Rose Foley for keeping my thoughts clear.

A special thank you to Marc Balara. Thanks for the TarHeel experience and belief in "the way of playing." It was all about the journey: the journey of respect, trust, accountability, and friendships.

To all the parents of all of the players I have ever coached who have given me endless life lessons and helped me on my journey to not only be a better coach but hopefully a better parent.

A sincere appreciation to Coach Harry Perretta for his passion and dedication to coaching the game of basketball for the past thirty-three years, for his constant generosity in sharing his system of plays and defenses with other coaches, and for his amazing knowledge of the game. A personal thank you to Coach Perretta for his endorsement of my book, *Parenting an Athlete*, and sharing his view of the role that parents play in their children's athletic careers.

TABLE OF CONTENTS

FOREWORD

As the head women's basketball coach at Villanova University for the past thirty-three years, I have experienced the evolution of basketball to its current state. The game has grown tremendously; travel and club teams have become more popular, and scholarships are more available. While this growth has opened new opportunities for athletes, it has also changed the expectations parents have for their children and for their children's coaches. In her book *Parenting an Athlete*, Annette provides expert insight into a trend that I have watched develop in recent years with much concern: parents becoming over-involved in the athletic development of their children.

In the past ten to fifteen years, I have watched an increasing number of parents play a bigger role in their child's athletic career. Attend a youth sporting event these days and you will see kids looking into the stands to their parents for advice, notice parents in the stands keeping track of their child's statistics and playing time, and hear parents blaming coaches and referees when their child performs poorly. As a parent of athletes first and a coach second, I realize the impact parents' actions have on their children. And like Annette, I wonder whether we, as parents, by becoming overly involved in our children's athletic careers, have lost perspective as to what sports are all about: teaching our children about life.

Annette does a great job in revealing the negative examples that over-involved parents are setting for their children. Most parents today, in order to shield their children from hurt feelings, blame coaches, referees, and other players when their child performs poorly. As a result, when children participate in athletics today, they learn to seek instant gratification and avoid responsibility instead of being patient and accepting accountability for one's actions. Also, many parents today tend to overemphasize individual statistics, such as shots, points, and playing time, and underemphasize team accomplishments. As a result, more and more children are learning selfishness and self-entitlement when participating in team sports instead of selflessness and commitment. As Annette points out (and I agree), most parents of athletes do not do this on purpose. No parent intentionally teaches their children to be selfish, irresponsible, and entitled. But by showing parents how their negative actions (and reactions) affect their children on the court, on the field, and in life, Annette helps prevent the bad consequences that often occur when parents become too involved.

Annette's book is great because not only does she highlight the problems created by over-involved parents but offers solutions as to how parents should act. Annette shows us that we as parents need to set good examples for our children in order for them to learn all of the life lessons sports have to offer. We need to teach kids to deal with their own problems. Everything is not always going to go well in life, and they have to be able to handle adversity. We need to teach our children that hard work, patience, and accountability are virtues that create character. We need to teach our children that experiences shared with others are more rewarding than individual statistics.

As an athlete and coach at the high school, college, and club level, and as a parent of a high school and college athlete, Annette is able to share experiences and insights that are of extreme importance and relevance to parents involved in athletics today. After reading Annette's book, I am more aware of the example I set for my two boys (fourth and sixth grade) as I watch them compete and develop as athletes. I am convinced that the lessons I learned from *Parenting an Athlete* have helped me become a better parent and a better coach and will help do the same for you. I encourage anyone involved in athletics to read Annette's book. You won't be disappointed.

—Harry Perretta
Women's head basketball coach
Villanova University

INTRODUCTION

The 2007 girls' basketball season was a turning point for me. I was an assistant coach of the South Jersey Tar Heels, an established Amateur Athletic Union (AAU) program. The coaching staff, as well as the parents and players, had high expectations for the season, which was designed to prepare the girls to compete at the next level of high school basketball. As coaches, we purposely went into the season looking to challenge the players. While basketball came easy to most of them, we wanted to stress intensity, leadership, collective responsibility, and accountability. What we did not plan for was the role of the parents' expectations that would change the course of the season. Had I finally had enough of parental influences—some negative attitudes and individual agendas—or would I stand up and attempt to make changes?

This book is my answer. Although I have been an AAU and high school coach for nearly twenty years, I am also the parent of an athlete, as well as a longtime athlete myself. While I have many experiences wearing all three hats, I have found it is most confusing and difficult being the parent of an athlete. I live and breathe with many other parents of this generation raising young athletes on the brink of high school sports and wanting so much for them to achieve and be at the top. I applaud parents for being so engaged in their child's life. We feel we know our child better than any coach and see the potential for success and possibly greatness. We have their best interest at heart. We would do everything in our power to help them and would not in any way want to stifle their development. I know this. I have lived this. And I continue to live it today.

But there is also a downside. What has become clear to me is while we as parents are trying to help our children, we may inadvertently be hindering them. We buy them the best equipment to participate in their sport. We send them to the best camps and clinics. We secure them personal trainers and private coaches. And why not? Hey, most of us were also athletes in our day, and we remember how it was. We were pretty good. But just think how good we could have been if our parents gave us more opportunities like the high school athletes of today—being sent to a variety of sports camps, playing our sport year-round in AAU programs, and providing us with personal trainers and the best equipment.

While none of these extras are bad—in fact they are necessary in the development of the child athlete today— we as parents have an even bigger role as a role model who maintains a positive attitude, no matter what the immediate situation. We need to be that parent who consistently feeds the child positive reinforcement and is able to spin adversity into a meaningful learning experience, that parent who allows their child to stumble and fall and then pick themselves up so potential growth can occur. We need to bite our tongue in the presence of our child, even when we feel they are being treated unfairly. If we continually voice negative comments, we provide the child an excuse, thus not allowing them an opportunity to find something in their own power to remedy the situation. I recognize that we, as parents, want so much for our child, but if we are willing to be patient and allow the child to figure some things out on their own and learn from mistakes, they will grow and develop both physically and emotionally.

Athletics is such a great avenue in learning life's lessons. Where else can you learn so much about what life is all about than being part of a team? You learn the skill of getting along with others, even if you do not like them. You learn how to deal with adversity and not let it change who you are. You learn to deal with unfairness at times. You learn the thrill of working hard to achieve your goals and also feel the disappointment of failure. If you are willing to get back up after you fall and work even harder, the rewards can be amazing. Sports give you the opportunity to learn about commitment, responsibility, adaptability, respect, selflessness, and trust. You also learn about pressure, emotions, friendships, rules, communication, and challenges.

So why do we as parents try to pave the path of our children in gold, only allowing the positive experiences to come into play? Why do we attempt to shield the adversities they may experience while participating in sports that inevitably could help them to grow and develop? This book examines those questions and others through relating my personal experiences as a player, coach, and parent, along with the experiences of other parents of athletes, as well as coaches and a family psychologist.

My hope is that in some small way this book will enable parents of child athletes to be better at parenting by aiding in the growth and development of their child and helping them become the best they can possibly be, both on and off the playing field. If this truly is our goal, then our attitude and our actions as parents will play a healthy role in the development of the athlete … our athlete.

2007 TAR HEEL SEASON...
A SEASON CUT SHORT

The Tristate Tar Heel girls' basketball season had started off so promising in 2007. So where did it go so wrong? What factors played a part in this season that demonstrated how parental influence can affect an entire team?

I look back now, and the girls, all of whom were twelve and thirteen-year-old junior high school students playing on an Amateur Athletic Union (AAU) team, were more than ready to take on everything we taught them: the plays, the defenses, the intense and organized practices. But in the end, our season was cut short, not because we did not qualify for Nationals, but because we, as coaches, could not hold this group of parents and players together as a team. We had taught the girls to become proficient with the Xs and Os, but we failed miserably in bringing this team together consistently. In the end, there was little unity between parents and coaches, which funneled down to the players, an important factor for any successful team. We may have looked good on paper, but we were not able to reap the benefits of this talented team, because we were not playing as a "team."

In the end, a few parents had had enough, did not understand the system and the playing time protocol, and threw away three more weeks of our team's and their daughters' potential learning, bonding, and invaluable preparation for high school and playing in a national arena. That was the saddest part.

Parents, through lack of communication by the coaching staff and their own lack of fundamental basketball knowledge, were confused, and became uneasy and offended by the coaches' decisions. I want to know how as coaches we could have avoided this and to what degree. Do we owe it to the parents to explain every move we make? Do we owe it to the players to explain everything?

I did not give the parents enough time to trust me, and, in their eyes, I changed everything from the previous season, including playing time, starting line-ups, and personnel. Looking back, I was wrong to think what I thought was a demonstration of the coaches' commitment the previous year when we went to Nationals was enough to compensate for any and all changes that were made during the 2007 season. That is what saddens, frustrates, and confuses me most. How can you make the parents, who are so influential with their child's attitude, trust and respect you without compromising your ways of coaching/ teaching?

Let us look at the season from the beginning. The coaching staff, along with the players and their parents, had high expectations for a successful season when it started in March 2007. And why not? We had just come off a thrilling Tar Heel season by competing at Nationals in July 2006. It was a great experience for the girls to be part of such intense competition at only twelve years of age and proved to be a social event for the girls and their families as well. Now these same girls—most of whom were in the middle of eighth grade in junior high school—were ready to learn skills that would prepare them to compete at the high school level in the fall.

Because I had sixteen years of high school coaching experience at three different schools in New Jersey, the head coach, Marc, looked to me as his assistant to help him prepare these girls for that coveted next level. We both saw that previous summer at Nationals the discipline and skill of serious basketball players, and we wanted that for our team. One parent in particular even asked, "What can we do? How can we get our girls to play at that level?"

I recognized that at age twelve, the game was still fun and a social event for some, but this was a key time for change, and it was the coach's responsibility to raise the level of teaching. While I am a true believer that the game should always be fun and it *is* just a game, I never wanted to compromise my beliefs that it should be played with heart, and it should also be taught with seriousness and respect. I knew we owed it to the players who wanted to take their game to that next level and compete in high school to give them everything we as coaches had in teaching them the game, the work ethic, and the skills.

We went into the season with a plan, wanting to challenge the girls. We knew we would frustrate some and take them out of their comfort zone, but all this would be a stepping-stone to bridge the gap to high school basketball. It would have been easier for us as coaches to ride the wave of that previous season and just have fun. But Marc, being a student of the game and wanting to learn as much as he could, wanted to prepare these girls and take the more difficult road. Although I took only a limited coaching role the previous year, Marc insisted I become involved with running my defensive/offensive system I had adapted at the high school level.

I was tentative at first to take on this added role, because I was burned out from experiences with parents at the high school level and the agendas for individual rather than team goals. I was also reluctant since I would be coaching my own daughter—something I stayed away from at all costs with my older daughter. I was firm in wanting my daughters to earn respect for their own talent and did not want others saying they played because their mom was the coach. Because I love to coach, and, more importantly, because I love to teach the game, I felt that being an assistant and having the role of preparing these girls for high school would be rewarding.

Because of a good turnout of potential players, tryouts were intense. We had enough girls to have two teams at this thirteen-year-old age group, so there would be an A and a B team. We ended up keeping only seven of the girls from the previous National team and chose three new girls. It was a grueling decision. We had spent hours of discussion with the four-member coaching staff in making these decisions and knew we owed it to everyone at the tryouts, not just our "Tar Heels," to be fair.

We began practices immediately and started teaching the girls at a new pace and level. Not everyone who plays eighth-grade basketball at the AAU level has a free pass to make their high school team, so our sights were set on preparing these girls for top-level play. Many of the girls also had aspirations of making the high school varsity team as freshmen. Based on the skills that I saw were lacking in their play, it was clear to me what we needed to teach and focus on as a team to bring everyone's game to a new level.

I applaud Marc, who had coached this team for two years previously and was willing to take a backseat at times so I could teach the girls a new way of not only playing but also practicing. We were teaching a match-up zone to thirteen-year-olds, and it was a hard concept to grasp. The match-up zone is a zone defense with man-to-man principles. The match-up zone defense entails a lot of communication among the defensive players, and to be successful, it takes all of the players working together as one. For the opposition, it looks like a man-to-man defense at times, which is confusing to the offense. And it is not an easy concept for junior high players to grasp.

We were also continuing with our motion offenses, which we introduced late that previous season. The coaching staff had a strong philosophy about how the game should be played. Since we firmly believed in the total team concept, I tried to instill that through my system of plays and defenses.

The players responded with amazing results. While I had never taught the match-up zone to girls this young, they did well with the concept, and we found success in the games. It confused many teams, not knowing if we were playing a man or zone, and it kept us in games where we were overmatched in size and talent. We continued with our strategy of teaching and understanding the bigger picture—that this was not just a one-year plan but also something we would build on as we moved forward. Marc had great insight into what he wanted these girls to learn, and although he did not have the experience as a high school coach or a system of plays and defenses, he had a clear vision of what needed to be done to take this team to a new level.

Marc and I spoke endlessly that season concerning the progress this team was making with learning the basic-yet-overlooked skills of moving without the ball, playing in the next minute, anticipating what will happen next, and learning to think and run complicated plays. Although we could see individual and team progress, it was not as evident from the outside, because we were not winning as many games early on as the previous years.

However, while we were thrilled with the intensity of the team's play at practice, we were becoming concerned with the level of play at tournaments midway through the season. We were baffled as to why at practice we were terrific running the plays, talking on defense, laughing, and smiling. The intensity level was high, and the girls were playing with passion and heart while having fun. And it was amazing to me how well we played as a team. At practice, though, no one was keeping track of who was scoring all the points. But as soon as it came down to the games, you might have thought we were an entirely different team. The focus became more on individual play and less of the team concept. Were players trying to please both the coaches and their parents?

You can argue that the games are different from practices because of playing time, and players and parents get frustrated if their child is not playing a lot. There was a lot of talk in the stands, complaints about the way the team was being run, the personnel, the starting lineup, the play calling, and the system. We as coaches initially thought the frustrations were stemming from the play of individual players. But we were wrong. We later found out that there were a few who were dissatisfied with all the changes we were making. There was little individual accountability, only excuses and finger pointing. We chose to ignore the comments and continue what we were doing, because it was clear to us that by following our plan to teach these girls a more complex system, they would develop into better and more knowledgeable basketball players.

Even with all the adversity, we felt we were progressing well, and by June, we were showing signs of being a competitive team for Nationals. We were receiving many compliments from other AAU coaches about our team in the discipline the players showed and the execution of the plays. However, I was still feeling ill at ease because I sensed a lot of these parents' fury was directed at me personally and, more distressingly, at my daughter Kristina.

Kristina joined the Tar Heels the season prior in 2006 and, being a quiet role-type player, did not stand out initially, so she got limited playing time her first season. This 2007 season meant a new season for her, and she knew she needed to step up her game and show her skills. When the season began, I do not think any parents initially thought of Kristina as a potential threat to their own child's playing time.

What was amazing to me was the transformation Kristina made going into this 2007 season. She had been frustrated with that previous season. She lost her confidence and did not like the role of a bench player at all. She had always been a go-to player, a starter, and a scorer on her other teams, and that negative experience had her motivated. Looking back, her attitude can be directly attributed to how my husband and I handled our frustrations during the 2006 season. Although I was tempted, we did not allow her to blame others for her playing time and frustrations. We tried to spin everything back to her role and what she could do to change the situation. Yes, I had to bite my tongue on many occasions because of my frustration with the situation. As a parent, my perception that year was that Kristina was not respected and was never given a chance in games. She was given only about two to three minutes at a time to do something and then was immediately taken out. In a few games, she never played in the second half.

My husband kept things in perspective, thank goodness, because I was on the verge at one particular tournament of becoming a "disgruntled parent" and voicing my opinion on the way home in the car in front of my daughter. And that is the mortal sin of parenting an athlete!

Instead, my husband and I had long discussions alone and decided Kristina may have an opportunity to learn many other lessons in this particular season. I desperately wanted her to play more. We felt she deserved to play more, but she would have to learn how to play with more urgency, to prove her worth to this team. She needed to learn how to enter a game and know she may only get a few minutes to do something positive and then be taken out. Okay, I thought, this was something new to learn. She was in unfamiliar territory with girls she just met, and even though she was only twelve years old, she now had a different kind of opportunity. It was not the opportunity to play a lot, but looking back now, it was an even better opportunity that could take her much further in life. Maybe it was not fair, we told her, but it was up to her to work harder to get what she wanted. And what she told us at the end of that 2006 AAU season made the whole season of frustrations much more bearable. She told us she could not wait to go back to her Catholic Youth Organization (CYO) team for her eighth-grade season and be a leader. She never appreciated how much playing time she received, and she now felt bad for the girls on her team who did not play much.

As a parent, I realized just how much Kristina grew as a player without "playing" much. I am thankful I had the wherewithal along with my husband's prodding not to base my daughter's growth and development in a season solely on playing time. I am thankful I knew through my experience of being a coach and being on that other side how much effect negative parents can have on a player. If I had voiced my opinion to my daughter when I was the most frustrated—and I came close—I would have given her an excuse for why she was not playing, and I would have funneled my bad attitude down to my child, thus not allowing her to take responsibility, have accountability, learn something, and try to make positive changes in her game.

Kristina came back to the Tar Heels for this 2007 season with amazing enthusiasm and passion to play. Prior to tryouts, she told me, "I can't wait to show the coach how much better I am." She had a mission, and she decided after her first season with the Tar Heels that she was a better player and wanted more playing time. So she took control of what she could and, in the off-season, practiced ball handling and shooting on her own. And she entered this new season with something to prove.

It was obvious to me from the 2006 season that the coach did not give the girls playing time just because their parent is a coach or keeps stats or because the player is his own daughter. He always plays those he feels are the best and should be out there. This was apparent in the case of Kristina. The coach now saw the positive change in her ability, and he began to play her more. She broke into the starting lineup. Kristina was not a flashy, go-to player on this team, but she hit shots consistently and always found the open girl. She did the little things that sometimes go unnoticed but make a difference, and the coach was now noticing her and the chemistry she brought to the team. Her minutes were up from the previous year.

I was pleased, but I sensed uneasiness within our team. I heard little things being said, and my fears were being realized. I knew Kristina had earned more time on the court because of her performance, but a few parents were crediting her increased playing time with my influence on the head coach as the assistant coach. A few were also unhappy with the style of play. So much was being said about how I was changing everything and confusing the players. We were told we were holding them back with all the new offenses and defenses and insisted we just "let them play."

Unfortunately, we knew we could not please everyone, especially each and every parent. We were making the girls accountable for playing time and teaching them to play in a system, all of which made some take a small step backward for a short time with the hope of taking that big leap forward. But unless the parents were positive and willing to buy into the system and the way we were coaching, their negative comments and attitude would affect their own child and potentially undermine the team.

Our biggest mistake was that we did not have a preseason meeting to explain what we were doing and what we were trying to accomplish. And in all fairness to the parents, we were changing what they had become used to without explanation. Life is one learning experience after another, and although I regret this mistake, it did teach me a lot about personalities, trust, respect, and the importance of not taking anything for granted. It taught me that parents could become easily frustrated and begin placing blame and making excuses for situations out of their control.

It became apparent to the coaching staff as the season progressed that some of the players stopped playing team basketball. In order to play at our highest level, we needed to play within the system, within the team concept of the game. There was an obvious internal struggle on whom to listen to … their parents or their coaches. If the negativity of the parents is expressed freely at home, this will confuse the player and potentially pull them away. Someone needed to be blamed, and I knew I was the obvious one because of the perception that I was responsible for all the changes—and to them, it was bad change.

We finally knew we had to make a decision about Nationals since a few parents were campaigning to end the season. We decided to have a parents' meeting during the last regular tournament to decide whether we should go to Nationals. I stood firm in wanting to go no matter what. I felt the girls earned it and should not be punished because of a few disgruntled parents. The meeting was long and brutal but productive. The parents agreed that if they knew why we were doing what we did, they perhaps would have accepted it better. It was interesting, because the parents of most of the players, including those who were getting little playing time, were thrilled with the season and the positive results of the hard work and diligence of the coaching staff in teaching the girls all the nuances of the game.

We did not go to Nationals in 2007, and although it was a successful season in terms of how much the girls learned, it was a disappointing year. But we as coaches realized in the end, we accomplished what we set out to do at the start of the season. Personally, I learned so much about myself and dealing with a variety of personalities that it was successful for my development as a coach.

The experiences of this particular season became the line I drew in the sand that made me even more passionate about the possibility of someday coaching a team that believed in the total team concept. I wanted to find the formula for the perfect team where team goals were primary and where accountability, trust, respect, and commitment to the team were second to none. It was at this point I knew I had to find a way to get the message out there about this crucial role parents play in the development of an athlete, specifically how negative attitudes, lack of accountability, and the blaming of others can stifle a player's growth and development. My experience tells me that no matter how much you deny it, parents play a big part in the success of the team and with their child's attitude.

LINDA MURPHY, parent of three high school athletes:

My concern is all the negativity by parents, not only toward the coaches and refs, blaming others, but the negative attitude to the players. I am concerned with the life-long insecurity issues they will have to live with forever. Athletics is only a small part of a child's life, and it will be done and gone, but the psychological issues will linger on for a long time. I am concerned that the athlete will look back and see that they were a disappointment to their parents, that they never really reached their full potential. Actually the potential that their parents saw in them. And maybe that was unrealistic.

KARYN PICKARD, high school basketball coach:

Over the years I have seen a drastic change in the attitude that parents take with sports. It is *ugly*! There is *hate* in the stands. It is just awful. I don't even like being a spectator anymore. There is venom in the tone of voice, there is hate directed at the coaches, there is violence directed toward the officials. 'Back when I played…' My mom came to every game. She watched us and enjoyed watching us. She raised five All-SJ athletes and she was humble. Never did she brag. Never did she complain to or about the coaches. Never ever did she say a word about the officiating. When the game ended, she told us good job. When the season ended, she thanked the coaches and offered them dinner at our house. She taught us character and accountability.

PLAYING BASKETBALL IN THE 1970s AND EARLY 1980s

After the 2007 season with the Tar Heels, I became obsessed with the role parents do play in the attitude of the child, which in turn affects the dynamics of the team. I was beginning to see an increasingly negative attitude with parents at games toward coaches, officials, and other players, and I yearned to fully understand in order to help me grow as a coach and become a better parent of my own athletes. I look back at my experiences as a player to understand the dynamics of parenting athletes in the '70s and early '80s. I reflect on how my parents taught and supported me in the intense competition of athletics.

JERRY CAMPBELL, former player in the 1960s, coach, parent, official:

Based on my experiences as a player, parent, coach, and basketball official, there are changes that are obvious and not necessarily for the good of the young athlete today:

- Parents' unrealistic expectations of their children's athletic ability.

- The myth of the 'college scholarship' opportunity.

- Structured venues for development (AAU, Camps, shooting/hitting coaches) have become huge profit centers. How much do they help, or does it just make parents feel good?

- Concentration on one sport, in reality, may diminish a young person's overall athletic development.

- National rating services of grammar school athletics. Another example of exploitation of athletics for a profit.

The advice that I would give to parents of high school athletics today would be to enjoy the ride; it will be over before you know it. Stay out of the way, and let kids be kids. Today, kids have adult supervision at home (hopefully), in school, and, in today's world, adult supervision at play. This time was supposed to be just for kids to be kids. Choosing sides, calling fouls, 'we have next game,' no trophies, no jackets, no adults. I'm afraid that a generation is growing up not experiencing 'just playing' the game.

ST. MARGARET'S, 1972-1975

I began playing the game of basketball at age ten when I was in the sixth grade. Back in the midseventies, basketball season was a winter sport played during a three-month period. I was excited to be on my school's Catholic Youth Organization, or CYO, team. We had a tryout, and there were cuts. Most of my classmates and local public school children who belonged to our parish participated. It was a pretty big deal to make the team. We practiced on Friday nights for two hours and on Saturday mornings from eight to eleven. We played about two games a week, sometimes on Saturday. I could not wait for the weekend to play basketball.

I did not find too much success that first season. I was just learning the game. I had natural athletic talent, but I did not know anything about the game and competing. I was playing against girls in sixth, seventh, and eighth grade. We as sixth grade players knew our place; we had to work for playing time, and usually the older girls were more skilled. Since I loved the game so much, I remember practicing on my own during the next summer on the small basket my dad had nailed above our garage. My older sister, Mary, who played for St. Margaret's three years earlier, and I would shoot hoops, play "horse," and practice. By the start of my seventh-grade season, I had improved greatly and became a starter on the team, and my career took off. At St. Margaret's, I had a wonderful gentleman as my first coach—Dan Adamski. He taught us the game, the rules, and how to be a good teammate and a good sport. He was always encouraging the players, and even though we were a competitive team, he stressed playing the game for the pure joy of competing. During my final year at St. Margaret's, we won the CYO championship, and I thought nothing could top that feeling. I also finally received that coveted first trophy.

I look back fondly at those formative years for me in athletics. It was a time when sports were, for the most part, only played in season. Sure, you would practice and play pick-up basketball in the off-season, but there were few AAU programs, few leagues, and little pressure to commit to only one sport and play it twelve months a year. We played sports for the joy of competition and to have fun. There were pressures, though, to make the team. There were few teams around, so you would have a sense of pride in knowing you made your school team. Yes, it was disappointing for those who did not make the team, but these players had two options: to practice and try to improve or move on to something else. There were no false pretenses that "everyone is good at the same talent level," and everyone has the right to play, no matter what. We learned life is not always fair and you were not handed everything just because someone complained to a coach, teacher, or an administrator. We received a trophy only if we won a championship, not just because we participated on a team. Our reward was "being on the team." There were expectations, but they were not unreasonable, and any disappointment I felt was usually directed at myself for not playing as well as I could have, rather than at a coach or referee. If I did not feel things went well for me, the only control I had was to do something about it by practicing and trying to do better next time.

I learned this attitude from my parents, who instilled in me the need to do better for the betterment of the team, not just for myself. Whether our team won or lost was more important than how I played as an individual. I was on a team, and team goals were always stressed. Coach Adamski would never allow a player to check the book after a game to see "how many points you had." I do not think too many of us even thought of that. It was always about St. Margaret's, the team. When your parents and coach instill this in you, it becomes the norm. I loved basketball, because to me it was the epitome of a team game—players working together for a common goal.

Let's talk about my parents' role and the role of most parents of my generation. My dad was my biggest supporter at this time. My mom was involved, but since I was the third child of five, she was busy running the household. My dad took me to practices, but both my parents came to every game.

My dad was intense, and he wore his passion for sports out on his sleeve. He grew up in South Philadelphia, and he loved sports—the thrill of competition. Although intense, I do know my father was a gentleman, and he was a fair man with great character. He taught me a lot about accountability. Even with his overzealous demeanor at times, I never can recall him placing blame on someone else for my play. He was willing to help me develop into a better player by taking me out to our little basket above the garage to "become better." He never gave me that easy out by placing blame on others for my poor performance, thus stifling my ability to improve.

I look back and have the utmost respect for and gratitude to my dad for being that role model who taught me that you must rise above adversities to be better than the next player. I can still hear him say, "No excuses. If you want it and it is not fair, then work harder than anyone else." What great advice for a young athlete, a young mind searching to find the answers, not just with basketball, but also with life. He was my role model, a great man, and a great father, who, through his own example of hard work, intensity, accountability, and extreme unselfishness, paved the way for me to learn how to succeed.

GLOUCESTER CATHOLIC HIGH SCHOOL, 1975-1979

As I entered Gloucester Catholic High School, I had no expectations for what basketball at that level of play would be like. I tried out for the freshman team and was moved up to junior varsity after the first practice. Since the JV and varsity players practiced together, I was able to learn so much from talented upperclassmen. I look back and realize I was fortunate for many reasons for having an intense and win-at-all-costs coach for my high school career. Within only a few games into the season, I found myself on the varsity bench. As the season progressed, I began to get a fair amount of minutes playing varsity.

Playing varsity on a state championship team brought a lot of anxiety, and I remember the intense pressure that year playing in a playoff game against Palmyra. It was late in the fourth quarter with the score tied when I was fouled on a rebound and had to walk to the other end of the gym, with screaming fans behind that basket to shoot a one-and-one. As I was walking toward the foul line, my coach called me over, grabbed my right arm, looked me in the eye, and said—and I will never forget this as long as I live—"Prove to me now why I moved you up to varsity as a freshman and have given you so much playing time, and make these foul shots." Wow, talk about scaring a kid! I kept hearing his voice as I walked to the stripe and had never felt such fear before. I made the foul shots, but I do not know if it was because I was afraid of the repercussions of missing or because I wanted to win so badly.

Unfortunately, my memories of high school basketball do not have many feel-good stories; it was all about competing and being the best we could be. We won four state championships, which I am proud of, but I spent four years playing a sport I loved afraid of my coach. Yes, he was intense and took a little of the joy out of the game for me, but I do feel he taught me how to be tough and never quit. I learned perseverance by playing for him. I learned to not let someone else dictate what I wanted to do. I wanted to play and he was the coach, so quitting was never an option. Now as a coach with all the adversities of dealing with parents and negative attitudes, this may be where I learned never to quit or compromise my beliefs and ways of coaching. I would not blame this coach or anyone else because of adversities I faced as a player. I learned well those four years that it was up to me to be the player I wanted to be, and even if "the coach" did not make it fun, then so what? I found a way to make it a positive experience.

I wanted to play the game, and it was up to me to make it what I wanted it to be. I learned the game, we played at an incredible level, and we won because we played as a team. My skills improved because of my coach, who taught me intensity and how to deal with failure and disappointment. Most of all, I learned respect and pride for my teammates. All this, the positives and negatives, helped to take me to the next level, not only for college basketball, but also for the competition of the classroom and, later on, for life.

What also was so key in my high school experience was the parental support given to all the players on the team. Every parent would cheer on every player whether they were starters or subs, whether they were the stars of the team, or players that rarely got in to the game. I recall the amazing support for the success of the team, not individual players. I truly felt other players' parents were also pulling for me. There was a "real" feeling in the air of being a part of a family… a team.

What is concerning to me now is that I just do not see much of this same attitude today. I see so much emphasis on individual goals and records. I see parents frustrated easily if their child is not playing well or taken out of a game. Why are we trying to pave the way for our children only in gold? We give them so many opportunities but then do not allow them to pick themselves up if they stumble and fall. Why do we make excuses if they do not live up to our expectations? We are so quick to blame others for failures when, in reality, what are failures? Are they really failures or just potential opportunities for real growth and knowledge? "Men succeed when they realize that their failures are the preparation for their victories" (Ralph Waldo Emerson).

In high school I learned to play hard and focus at all times; all of this added to my already intense personality. I learned to take criticism and use it to make myself better. I did not realize until my experiences as a coach that two things can occur with a player's response to coaching instruction, whether it is perceived as teaching or criticism. A player can work harder to make themselves better, or they can quit. The player has no control over the coach; therefore, if a player uses the coach as a tool for self-improvement no matter what is said and uses the coach's words, either positive or negative, as motivation, then the player has the potential to come out on top. And isn't that the goal?

I know this is the perfect scenario of a player with confidence ignoring a negative and intense coach and using it to grow and develop. I realize when we talk about children who are ten, eleven, and twelve years old that this is difficult to do. It is the responsibility of the coach to be a positive teacher, but this is not always the case. Therefore, I encourage parents to allow their child to see the positive side of all coaches, especially youth coaches. Some parents think a coach has an agenda and is only coaching to promote and develop their own child. Whether this is true or not, it is important not to feed these feelings to your child, the player. Even in the worst-case scenario, a player still has an opportunity, even if it is the smallest, to develop as a player if parents promote positive thoughts and never allow the player to harbor negative thoughts and potentially harmful perceptions that will stifle a player's development.

There is a learning opportunity in every experience, so be careful not to throw away potential opportunities to grow. I look back and realize that my high school coach provided me with avenues for learning and developing. At the time, I did not know how much I was learning, not only about all the nuances of basketball, but real life as well.

Sports are a reflection of life's lessons, and we need to embrace this. If you only looked for positive experiences in sports, then you would be missing out on greater learning opportunities. Your child would be unprepared for adversity, and what lesson would that be in preparing your child for real life? It is during these adversities that the real learning, growing, and developing take place. That is why I find it perplexing that parents continually try to deflect potential learning opportunities from their children by blaming others and denying their children accountability. The players' destination is in their own hands, and this is proportional to the players' attitude.

My experience of playing high school basketball and having parents who instilled in me accountability provided me the opportunity to make myself better through perseverance. I played because I wanted to, because I loved the game. I learned and grew because it was hard. No one made it easy for me. There were no short cuts, and, fortunately for me, there were never any excuses. It was up to me; it was my deal. And what a great life lesson basketball was for me. I am so passionate about sports, coaching, and teaching the game because of these early experiences. I learned not just the ways of playing, but much more importantly, I learned the ways of living because of the positive attitude of my parents.

BRAD WARD, father of high school soccer and basketball player:

I always felt it was very important for the child to be responsible for addressing any issues with the coach. Any issues concerning playing time, practice, and game situations, etc., should be between player and coach. I didn't want to offer any of my own opinion that would influence my daughter. I wanted my daughter to form her own opinions and deal with any issues with coach or teammates on her own. I feel that is very important. I'm sorry to say that in my opinion, these days, parents have *no problem* approaching the coaches or an AD and offer opinions and sometimes demand certain things of the administration. I have seen it since the time she was six years old, and it has continued through high school. I'm hoping it doesn't continue in college, but it wouldn't shock me.

COLLEGE EXPERIENCE, WIDENER UNIVERSITY, 1979-1983

There is so much to learn about life through a college experience, not just in the sporting arena, but also in the classroom and campus life. My mother taught me early in life and continues to teach me that a person should never stop learning and growing—each stage in life is a perfect opportunity to become more knowledgeable and allow your mind to grow and experience something new. College was that time for me where I experienced adult life lessons of extreme joy and pain, disappointment, failure, and achievement. I found true love, and I experienced death firsthand, all within four months. I met my husband the summer going into my sophomore year of college in 1980, which brought me pure happiness. But my father, my number one fan, was battling cancer and died that December.

I look back at that time in my life, and yes, it was difficult; it was tragic for my family and me. My father and I had a special relationship, and I know how much he loved me; I know how much he wanted to teach me in the short time he was in my life. Although none of us knew it at the time, he was able to give to me, in those formative years, knowledge and experiences I could use for a lifetime. It is thirty years later, and his approach to athletics and raising an athlete was so correct and insightful. He allowed me to be accountable for my actions and always insisted on commitment. He allowed me to experience disappointment and failure, not always shielding me from a perception of unfairness, to allow me to live and experience the good and the bad at that early stage in life. I look back at my college years, the years on the doorstep to adulthood, where my parents prepared me well for life.

I had a successful college career on the court, but looking back at my college years, the years on the doorstep to adulthood, my success in playing college basketball brings back only minute memories compared to what I learned through my experiences, friendships, and the knowledge I gained in the classroom. When you are going through a life experience such as college or playing high school and college sports, you feel it is an enormous portion of your life, and you put so much emphasis on it. But it is important that parents not get so caught up in athletics and have a disproportional emphasis on it that they lose perspective and miss out on the entire college experience of not only athletics but academics, friendships, successes, and failures … real life's lessons.

BRAD WARD, parent of athletes:

In my opinion, parents also need to understand the definition of "student athlete." The primary focus of all athletes should be on their academics. If you are a good student first, any athletic achievements will be icing on the cake. Academics are the key to the future. A devastating injury can put any athletic endeavor in jeopardy, but if you have good grades, you'll always be successful. As adults and parents, we need to be positive role models and set a good example for our child athletes.

I have observed parents getting so uptight with the sport, with their child playing, anticipating good and bad and not enjoying the moment. Some have verbally expressed the pressure of watching their child play and projecting what will happen. They worry their children are not developing enough. They are not getting enough playing time, the coach is calling the wrong plays for the good of their child's development, or others are shooting too much, taking away from their child. They worry about the position they are playing, because in college, which may be five or six years away, they need to be in a particular position to play at the college level. All the while, they are missing out on the present, the joy of watching their child "just play." They want it to be something else, so they deny themselves the present and all it has to offer.

I know seasons fly by and careers pass all too quickly. You think high school goes by fast, but college becomes only a blur. It frustrates me to see parents always looking to the future and not appreciating the here and now. I realize their need to prepare and have a plan, but if preparing denies you joy of what is actually taking place—what your child is achieving *now*—then that is tragic. I have had parents later tell me how sorry they are now because they missed so much by churning when the actual joy was at that particular moment and they missed it. It reminds me of lyrics in John Lennon's "Beautiful Boy" song: "Life is what happens to you while you're busy making other plans."

To this day, I continue to play the game I love so much and has, in so many ways, identified me. At age forty-nine,

I find it hard to compete at the level I once knew, but I find it fulfilling to just work out and shoot with my daughters, playing one-on-one or two-on-two, and even attempt to play in a summer league. My days are numbered in playing competitively, but who would have ever imagined that in the 1970s at age ten when I first began playing that thirty-nine years later the game would still be a big part of my life? Basketball has brought me so much in life, not only as a player, but also as a coach. I hope now through coaching and teaching the game that I am giving back just a small portion of what this sport has given me.

KARYN PICKARD, high school coach:

While I played high school and college sports, I never really thought about how special our parents were "back" then. But as I look back and I think about it, I have nothing but fond memories of my mother sitting in the stands or in the bleachers. I know that I was aware of her presence at all of my games. The picture back then was parents in the bleachers supporting the team and their own child. Team came first. They were separated from us by the boundary of the court/field. They never got overly involved. They respected the opponent, coaches, and officials (even if a bad call was made), and in return, taught us so much by just sitting there appreciating the competitive nature of both teams and accepting the outcome of the game. An amazing concept that is all too forgotten today. I was recently at a boy's basketball game and witnessed firsthand the head coach's family yelling at the officials during the entire game. It was awful. Thirty-two minutes of ripping the ref. Not one administrator said a word. There was so much hate directed at the officials that it brought me down. It was a big game, and it should have been a positive experience, but it was ugly. The adults act this way, and the "kids" watch and "cock" their heads in confusion … that's what it has become! I feel fortunate to have played sports when it was so much easier. I often think that I would have more opportunities today versus the time frame that I participated. However, I would not want to be an athlete today with the way people treat "sport." I feel fortunate to have fond memories of the competition and the "smell" of the gym. I have fond memories of every second I competed on the court and field. I loved life when I was practicing or playing the game. That sound of your sneakers on the floor and the feel of your lungs burning made me realize that I was an athlete. There was a desire to win, and great efforts were put forth to accomplish your goals. Those efforts happened in the backyard or down at the playground, not necessary in an organized structure with parents attending. It was through pride that you made it happen. Never did you want to rotate off. I am not sure that kids today are afforded the privileges that we experienced by just going outside and making up games. Kids today do not get the opportunity to develop that intestinal fortitude, because if you don't make a team, daddy is going to complain and maybe fix it for you and get the coach fired. Makes for a weak world, if you ask me.

MY PERSONAL EXPERIENCES AS A HIGH SCHOOL COACH

I began coaching in 1990, and I became aware early on in my coaching career of the influence parents have on their child, which funnels down to the team. I look back at my early years of coaching and realize the attitude of parents slowly became more and more intense with each year, each season I coached.

The ultimate question for a coach often is: What is the difference between teaching and criticism? Or better yet, how do you condition parents and players to understand that teaching a nuance of the game is not criticism? If a parent perceives that their child is constantly being criticized, then inevitably that perception will inhibit their child's learning process. Good coaching should always begin and end with good communication, which can prevent such perceptions. It is vital that the coach establishes himself as a teacher of the sport and the basketball court as an extension of the classroom. A coach needs to consistently demonstrate that coaching is, in fact, teaching the game and aiming to improve each player's skills in order to become a strong team. With an open mind—first by the parent, then by the player—that welcomes instruction, the door is open for growth and development.

MARC BALARA, parent, girls' AAU and boys' grammar school coach:

Being a coach and being a parent can sometimes work together nicely, but sometimes work against each other. A coach is logical, analytical, motivational, and in control of the totality of the team, and sees all aspects of what is happening on the court. A parent is emotional, unconditional, and controls nothing, and is limited to seeing only what their child is doing well or not well. We as parents have expectations going into the season, and I think this is where we all fall into a trap. I've tried to learn not to expect anything, but anticipate everything. I also think one of the greatest difficulties is that it is not me playing down there, no matter how much I would like it to be…it's my daughter, and she is responsible and accountable for her play, not me, not the coach, not her teammates. When she plays well, she plays well…not me. When she plays bad…she plays bad…not me. But then why do I feel elated when she scores the winning basket and crappy when she turns the ball over…I'm a parent; I love her, and when our kids hurt we hurt, when our kids rejoice we rejoice; it's a normal "parenting side effect." The key, however, is not playing the "blame game"; she is accountable for her play, no one else. I will not get trapped by blaming anyone else for how my child plays. Maybe this is my coaching experience talking, but in the end it is just a game, and if she is happy, healthy, having fun ... and oh, doing great in school ... there are no issues at all. My children's careers have been filled with adversity, success, disappointment, and joy ... sounds a lot like life.

GLOUCESTER CATHOLIC, 1990-1997

My first coaching experience was with the 1990-1991 Gloucester Catholic Lady Rams freshman team. I was asked to coach the team by my sister, Lisa, who had just finished her first year at Gloucester Catholic High School as the freshman coach and was now moving up to become the varsity girls' head coach. Although I knew the game of basketball as a player and was excited to coach, I had no coaching experience. I did come in with a coaching philosophy, though. I wanted all of the girls to get adequate playing time, but I also wanted the freshman program to be competitive. Consequently, although every girl played in each game, the better and more talented players earned more playing time. I wanted the players to know and understand competition, play hard, and be committed to the team but also have fun playing the game. I knew, for most of these girls, their days playing organized basketball were numbered, and I wanted them to go out with fond memories.

I remember this time of coaching as being a happy time. I had little experience handling players, personalities, and parents; yet fortunately, I had few problems. Parents were happy to see their child playing high school basketball and appreciated that their child got into the game. We were a competitive team, and we won most of the games. It was a great learning experience for me. It was also a good time in my life to start coaching. My children were two and five years old and not yet in school. Since I worked full time as a visiting nurse and had been working with my company since 1984, I was well established in my job and could take on all the demands of coaching a freshman team.

During my second season of coaching, I moved up to the junior varsity team, which put a lot more demands on my time. We practiced every day with the varsity team. I was now in a great situation to learn so much about running an efficient practice. Lisa, the head coach, ran the practices, which were outlined with exact time frames. Such organization kept practice moving swiftly and proved to be efficient. We covered everything and I saw firsthand how much the players were learning. I also saw how receptive they were and how the players remained engaged in the practice, which is key. I learned how to scout a game and go over a scouting report with the players. I learned so much from Lisa, whom I consider one of the best coaches in the area.

For the next six years, I coached at the junior varsity level. Because I have always loved competition and the excitement of the game, I enjoyed having my own JV team, but I also liked sitting on the bench of the varsity games as an assistant coach. I remember being conscious of not playing at all costs but instead teaching sportsmanship and fairness. I wanted everyone to play in every game, but I do remember a few games where this was not possible. I wanted to be competitive, and at this level, it was important to play to win.

The better players, some of whom suited up for the varsity team, needed more playing time to develop. The players basically understood this philosophy, but it did not go over well at times, and I had my first experiences of handling adversity. I learned an incredible amount from Lisa, including her system of motion offenses and the match-up zone. It was a great opportunity for me. I could not have written a better script for starting off my coaching career.

There were only a few parenting issues during my tenure at Gloucester Catholic. There was that common scene with parents approaching the coach and questioning why their child did not make the team or why their child was not playing as much as they thought they should. One particular parent, whose daughter was cut from the team, was very upset. When the head coach tried to be nice and explain to the parent that she could only keep a certain number of players, the parent actually offered to buy more uniforms so his daughter could stay on the team. While this sounds like a cute little story, it actually is a good example of how engaged parents are in the lives of their children. Parents want so much for their child that "they" are willing to do what it takes. Do we as parents really think we can step in and possibly fix any situation for our child?

Another more serious parenting issue involved an extremely talented player. What was most memorable about this particular player was the intense attitude of her parent concerning her play on the court. It was always about how she was performing as an individual. Every play and every decision was critiqued and not in a quiet manner.

Her freshman year was uneventful, and there was good chemistry with her out on the court. As she developed during her sophomore and junior year, it was clear she was our go-to girl, and the whole team revolved around this player. Her parent now became even more critical of every move she made. I remember thinking what a great player she was and how proud I was of her play, but her father vocalized so many negative comments—from yelling at the refs and screaming and yelling at his daughter to eventually criticizing every move the coach made. I began to feel sorry for this player with the intense pressure she must have been feeling to please her father.

The focus of her senior season became all about individual records, and this went against everything Lisa and I stood for in our coaching philosophy. Lisa said many times that individual goals are always secondary to team goals. The irony is, between us, we had seven high school state championships as players. We knew the thrill of winning as a team far outweighed individual awards.

"I would have traded my scoring record back then for that fourth state championship," Lisa would say. Many of today's players fail to understand the joy and accomplishment that is felt winning a "team" championship.

This player went on to win numerous individual awards. I look back now and know this talented player could have had all those individual records and probably more, along with a team championship. She started out her freshman year with lots of enthusiasm, respect, and team play. But as the years went on, the focus was on individual records. I could feel the pressure on everyone, and it truly was a sad situation. I cannot help but think that if the emphasis had been on team rather than individual goals, she could have broken many more records sooner.

JULIE McHENRY, high school softball coach:

Over the years, parents have become more and more involved in their children's athletic pursuits. I realize that most parents want to give their child every opportunity to excel, but sometimes it is just too much. Many times, girls would leave our softball practice only to be dragged to pitching lessons, hitting lessons, or to another practice for one of their other teams. I say dragged, because most of the time it was obvious that it was something that they did not want to do. I had several parents take their daughters straight to the batting cages after every game that they did not perform well in. Dinner would have to wait. Homework would have to wait. I remember one instance where our pitcher was so happy because her Amateur Softball Association (ASA) team was finally not scheduled to play on the weekend, only to find out that her dad had promised another team that she would be a "guest" pitcher for them. I once had a player come to me in tears after a game and ask me to "call a meeting" so that she would not have to drive home with her father and hear about how terrible she had played that day. I have had my entire team ask me to forbid them to play for other teams during our state tournament so that they would not have to go to their ASA practices or tournament games during that time. I have had parents attend not only every game of their daughter's softball career but many, many, practices as well. I have had parents who made their daughters (unwillingly) transfer to other schools because they were not starting for our team. I even had a starter transfer because she was not pitching every game.

I have also had many parents over the years that I considered to be the "perfect" softball parents. They showed up at every game and cheered on their daughters and the team. Good game or bad, their attitude remained positive, encouraging, and supportive. Their emotional well-being was not dependant upon how their daughter performed that day.

I believe there is a fine line between being a supportive parent and being "over the top." Many of my players with the most demanding parents were the best players I ever coached. But at what point does being supportive cross over to being controlling and manipulative? Many of my former players continued to play and love the game of softball, but some of them stopped playing because of the pressure their parents put on them. I had one very talented player who stopped playing her senior year because of the effect her game had on her entire household. She said, "When I play well, everything at home is great, and when I play poorly, all hell breaks loose." I try never to forget this girl and what she said when it comes to being a parent of my own child athlete. I have been very cautious when dealing with my own daughter. I have tried not to push her too hard and have avoided putting her in the position of "burning out" at a young age. She did not start playing AAU basketball until last year at the age of thirteen. Even then we were careful to find her a team that would both enhance her skills and provide her with an opportunity for fun and new friendships. She has had a very positive experience both with AAU and high school ball and now realizes what is required to be a student-athlete at the high school level. As a parent, I can recommend and financially provide for ways for her to improve her game, but only she can decide whether she has the heart and the desire to do so.

GLASSBORO HIGH SCHOOL, 1997-2000

I accepted my first head coaching position at Glassboro High School in June 1997. I was like a deer in headlights, eagerly waiting to make my impact as a coach in the sport I loved. I was flooded with ideas on how I wanted this team to play. I had enough enthusiasm for the whole team. What I would soon find out was that I had all the eagerness and demonstrated it outwardly, while the players seemed noncommittal. This was a rude awakening for me as a coach. I had an early meeting with the players before the school year let out to introduce myself and discuss ideas about the upcoming season and summer league. The girls were apprehensive.

I realize now, thirteen years later, I probably scared the players with my intensity. I had my mind set to teach them the game the way I knew it and how I wanted it played without first finding my starting point. I came from Gloucester Catholic, where the players eat, drink, and sleep basketball. I quickly learned it is not like that everywhere. Looking back now, I realize a coach should first assess the situation and then get to know the players—find out who they are, where they come from, and any experience they may or may not have playing the sport. A coach needs to get to know the make-up of the group of players he or she will be coaching/teaching.

My experience at Glassboro was second to none. Unfortunately, I did not come to realize that until I left the school and moved on. The program at Glassboro taught me wins and losses and coaching basketball were secondary when you have the opportunity to teach life lessons. I learned from these kids as much as I hopefully taught them. I realized in the big picture these girls were dealing with outside issues that were distracting, and although basketball was at the top of my priority list at this time in my life, it was way down the scale for most of the girls. But what the players showed me was once they learned the fundamentals, sportsmanship, and basic nuances of the game and played with the commitment and enthusiasm I demanded, positive play resulted. I saw, with a little direction, these girls began to take pride in their team, and a commitment was established. It was not all perfect, but with that constant reminder of teaching them pride, respect, enthusiasm, trust, and how to handle disappointment and failure, they grew as players and as a team.

As I look back at my three-year tenure at the school, I am not always proud of how I handled every situation. I realize now my level of intensity scared some of the girls and made them feel self-conscious. There were many lessons to be learned by me as a new coach, as well as by the players. I realize I want to take away not only all of my positive coaching experiences that were effective in teaching these girls, but I want to remember the mistakes I made so as not to repeat them.

My respect for these girls came with watching their journey as they learned the system and "my way" of playing and then adapting. They wanted to please and succeed, even if the way I was teaching the game took them out of their comfort zone. I realize now I was asking them to do something foreign. But they responded well.

In the end, I experienced players elevating themselves and their game without many of the opportunities we take for granted. These kids had heart, and although I thought they might not be working hard enough, they were working as hard as they could. From my vantage point today, I find great pride in what we all accomplished as a team and as individuals. We did not win many games, but we won on many other different levels. These girls became successful in respect to accountability and attitude. They set goals and worked hard to achieve them.

I found out later when running into a former player who was working at a nursing home that she decided to enter the health profession. She came running up to me— it had been ten years since I had last seen her—and she seemed excited to talk. She still called me coach, which brought a big smile to my face, and she shared her goals with me. An ordinary day turned into a top-ten day of my life. The rewards of coaching this team came flooding into my heart and made me appreciate that I was the luckiest person around. I realized, wholeheartedly, it is better to give back to the sport without any expectations of game success. And then when you least expect it, the real gifts and fruits of your labor come rushing back to you tenfold.

I stayed at Glassboro for only three years and when I met with the team just after the 2000 season to try to explain why I was leaving and moving on to Bishop Eustace, one particular player, probably my most talented player, stormed out of the meeting, angry and disappointed. On her way out, she said she was quitting basketball. I tried to talk to her but she left quickly. I left sad, questioning my motivation for leaving this team.

I rationalized that I was leaving because I thought I had a better opportunity to coach a premier program in the area and deep down I knew it would be more challenging coaching in a better conference. But what was I really about? Was I being selfish, looking out for my own interests when in only three short years I had established something special with this team, this program that needed consistency and commitment? I preached to these girls day in and day out about life, perseverance, and commitment. And now where was my commitment? I did not expect this reaction from the players. They truly did become my players, and now I was leaving. I worked hard for this team, as did they, and on my way home, I questioned my character. A few days later, one of the players, Sheemea, sent me a letter. She was outwardly a tough girl who refused to show personal emotions. But I knew better and I was sorry to be disappointing her. She told me she understood and she also had goals. She promised to make me proud. Her letter is one of my greatest possessions as a coach.

Coach,

Hi, how are you doing? Me, I'm fine, but still a little mad and hurt. I know you're probably saying, "Why in the world is she writing me?" Well, the reason why I'm writing you is because I had to write you to get this out of my head and I couldn't tell you this face-to-face. It was very hard for me and the rest of the team when you said you weren't coming back next year. We thought you were just coming in to talk to us about summer league of some kind of camp. I know you were wondering why I left the room like that. Well, the reason I left was because I was about to cry. I really felt like my basketball career was over.

I say that because when I walked into that first meeting at the beginning of my freshman season, I

thought, *I'm really going to like this coach*. I mean, you
made a lot of sense to me from the little bit that you
were saying. Then when I played that year, I learned
a whole lot from you. When I started in seventh and
eighth grade, it was just a hobby for me. The only
reason why I played in high school was to see if I
was going to make something of this sport. To tell
you the truth, I didn't even know all the calls. The
only thing I knew was how to shoot and foul people.
But because of you, I learned a lot about the game. I
really want to thank you for that. The first time I got
on your bad side as a freshman, I thought you would
just give up on me. But you didn't; you still helped
me and never gave up on me. Even after that, I still
got on your bad side sometimes. I know if you were
any other coach, I would have been kicked off the
team a long time ago. That's how I knew you really
cared about me and the other girls. I used to come
home after every practice and tell my mom what a
great coach you were and how much fun I was having
learning the game. Then there were some days when
I was mad and would go home and tell her that I
didn't want to play for you anymore and I quit. Then
I would think about what a wonderful coach you
were and change my mind about quitting.

I know you really cared about me and what my
game was going to be like. I say that because there
were times when I couldn't do anything right in
practice or times when I just didn't care. Now I regret
that because you are gone now.

I thank you most because of what you helped me do my sophomore year. Because of you, my game reached a whole other level—from my passing, shooting, and defense and the little bit of leadership I have, but most of all, my confidence, self-respect for others. I bet after you suspended me, you thought I would never get any better. After that time, I knew that you were at the end of your rope and was about to kick me off the team, so I straightened up. From that time, I grew as a person and learned to respect people and other's feelings a lot more. I know my game improved a lot from that point because my attitude was better and I became a better leader. I just wish you had done that sooner, but I also know I should have had a better attitude from the start. But every person has to grow.

Most of all, I wish I could have made the playoffs for you, but we tried hard; we only fell a little short. I just hope that your change will be a change for the better. Now I can see why you are leaving, but the main thing I know is you loved all of your players. I'm not writing so you will come back. I'm writing you to say thank you for all that you have done for me and Glassboro High. If it's that next step you need in life, go for it. I know that when it's time for me to take that next step, I'm going to do it and owe it all to you. You changed some parts of my life all the way around in the two years that I've known you. All that you taught me, I'm not going to let it go to waste. I'm going to use it to the best of my ability. I just ask that you won't forget about me or the other players. And we hope to see you at some of our games. Also, any advice that you have for us, please tell us. I will be sure to call you if I have any questions or need somebody to talk to. We will never forget you. I hope you never forget us. Good luck, Coach. I bet they will love you as much as we love you. Tell your kids that we said hi. Thanks for everything.

Your #1 point guard,
Sheemea Carr

Sheemea did not quit playing basketball, instead continuing her career at Rowan University. I was able to watch her play some games at the college level. She continues to be a great inspiration to me as a coach. Glassboro may not have brought me the most success on paper, but it truly was one of my greatest gifts. It is never about just wins and losses. Sports should be about so much more.

This experience at Glassboro is important in understanding the role the Glassboro parents played. I did not have any disgruntled parents in the stands. The parents that attended the games supported their daughters and the team, some louder than others. My entire focus was given to the team, to the players. Looking back now, it was a breath of fresh air to see the players' focus was on playing, the coach's focus on coaching, and the parents sitting and cheering for the team—a great concept.

BRAD WARD, parent:

The one thing my wife and I always stressed to both of our children was the *effort* that they put forth. We always told them that they owe it to themselves, their teammates, and their coach. Missing a shot, making an error, making any kind of mistake is acceptable; nobody is perfect. In sports, someone is going to win and someone is going to lose, and sometimes, things happen in games. I always told them both, the only thing that a player can control is their effort. Dealing with all the other things that can happen in a game is just part of the game. Hustle and effort are the most important things when competing. If you had asked me prior to my daughter's high school career, I would have told you that her teams she competed on would win a couple championships, and if they did, I felt she would be recognized individually. We all had high expectations. Unfortunately, due to injuries, she was unable to attain the goals that I'm sure she had set for herself. That said, coming back from those injuries taught her many valuable lessons and increased her love for the sport. Sometimes you don't realize what you have until it is taken away from you. Often, people take things for granted. I believe that was the case with my daughter. She was able to turn a negative situation (being injured) into a positive and has come back stronger than ever.

I learned very early that many parents have unrealistic expectations of coaches, teammates, and referees and of their own children. While most are positive and supportive of their own children and the rest of the team, some parents are always negative, embarrassing, screaming at players, coaches, referees, the opposing players and fans, or anyone that will listen to their nonsense. I'm sorry to say this behavior is very prevalent in high school and youth sports in 2010. With each passing year, parent behavior has become more and more unacceptable than previous seasons. I'm not sure where it will end up or what the future brings in this area, but something needs to change.

BISHOP EUSTACE, 2000-2005

Leaving Glassboro High School was an emotional decision, but I knew it was the right one for me from a coaching standpoint. Although Bishop Eustace was not a powerhouse, in my mind, there were great possibilities and opportunities for me in furthering my coaching résumé. I was anxious to start a new chapter in my coaching life. Bishop Eustace had a good reputation and a star player that was a legitimate Division I recruit.

I entered this new arena and was amazed at the possibilities. My whole system, my offenses and defenses, revolved around the team aspect. The coach who preceded me was well respected. Although I knew little about her system, I needed to implement my system, my way of playing the game, immediately. I realize with any change, a period of adjustment was needed.

I felt immediate resistance from some of the parents, which was expected. Losing a well-liked coach was difficult for some players and parents. As with any coaching change, some of the players now had to change the way they had become accustomed to playing. I insisted on teaching every aspect of the game to make every player better. I knew especially if my star player were to play at that next level, a Division I college, she would need to improve each skill and understand every nuance of the game. I knew the benefit of a center being more versatile in preparation for the college game.

At the time, I knew little about parents and the impact they have on their child. I wanted to do everything in my power to help each player reach their ultimate potential at both the high school and possibly college levels. But I am not so sure this was possible due to the resistance I felt from a few parents regarding the system of play I had implemented. I do not feel there was enough time those first few years to gain the trust and respect by the parents. I came in as a new coach, made many changes, and met resistance. It funneled down to the players, which, in turn, funneled down to the team. I cannot help but wonder if a positive attitude from the beginning between parents and coach would have allowed us to find more success that first season.

There were many similar stories of disgruntled parents during my tenure at Bishop Eustace. In reality, it was that same old story everywhere, with parents trying so hard to give their child every opportunity to succeed in the only way they knew how. It was about parents being so emotionally involved and doing everything in their power to see that their child succeeds, many times at the expense of the team. It was also an era where I saw many players transferring to different schools because they felt there were better opportunities in a different arena and with a different coach. But as I looked around the various leagues and followed these players who had transferred, I wondered if the transfer really helped the players reach their potential and fulfill their own personal needs.

I was fortunate, although there were a few unhappy and rebellious parents, I had a great group of parents who supported the team and their daughters. In retrospect, I had little adversity with parents compared to what I am seeing today. But with each year I was at Bishop Eustace, the parent/player issues became more intense.

In 2002, my second year at Bishop Eustace, we won the Parochial B State Championship. This particular team had the right combination of talent and excellent work ethic. At the start of the season, our goal was to win "states." I realized early on the potential these players had. I wanted these players to have that feeling of accomplishment and pride I had experienced as a high school player in the late 1970s winning a state championship. What I did not expect was the personal satisfaction I felt winning a state championship as a coach. It was far more rewarding winning as a coach than as a player. I was happy for my players and their parents to be a part of a championship team. The season had its ups and downs, but in the end, it finally *was* all about the team—coaches, players, parents, not individuals. It all came together in March 2002.

I experienced with each new season more and more expectations from the parents with each of their daughters. I saw more and more emphasis placed on individual goals and less on the team aspect. I always have been a firm believer of team goals coming first, but it was getting harder and harder to pull everyone into this philosophy.

I loved coaching at Bishop Eustace, but family was always my first priority. I decided to step down in 2006 to watch my own daughters play basketball and support them. I no longer was the coach making the decisions—I now became the parent full time. I soon realize this job of "parenting an athlete," with all the emotions, truly is the hardest job of all.

MARC BALARA, parent:

I think we as parents over think/over analyze, "If I just tell her this one more thing…" and I think after a while, although I think I'm being helpful, I might just be another parent with too much to say that's not necessary. My daughter listens every time, but I know she is just being polite; I should just let her be. I do not think this has hindered my daughter per se, but I think it can become more like work than a game…a "parental press conference" that she has to attend after every game. Heck, the professional coaches and players do not like postgame press conferences…why should a fifteen-year-old like one or have to attend one … after every game? I'm getting better at this, I think.

I love watching my kids play, I love watching them work hard, I love watching them succeed, I do not love watching them fail … but I love what can come from their failure … the ability to overcome, learn, and understand. This is where I choose to focus my energy; we all perform less than we are capable sometimes, and sometimes we perform exactly what we are capable of … the key is to learn, have fun, and work as hard as you can. It's in the working hard that matters, that builds your ethic for reaching your potential in whatever you do. The best commercial on TV is the one that shows all these great college athletes who will never go on to play professional sports, but they will be stars in the professions they do choose outside of sports. Education is the winning shot every time, working hard is the key rebound, and passion for what you love is the championship. If my kids learn this, then everything else is just a two pointer.

2008 TAR HEEL SEASON ...
THE PERFECT SEASON

After looking back and reflecting about parenting attitudes with my own parents and parents of my teammates twenty-five to thirty years ago, I see a different approach most parents took in the '70s and '80s. I also see clearly now a pattern with each year I coached at the high school level and then with AAU. With each passing season, I experienced increased parent interference affecting the morale of the team, leading up to that disappointing 2007 Tar Heel season. My internal struggles dealing with parents' attitudes made me all the more motivated and obsessed with coaching that perfect team. That team that could exist with harmony among the players, parents, and coaches—a team where parents actually cheer for the entire team and support the coaching staff in the name of the team and not individual agendas. So at the start of the 2008 Tar Heel season, the coaching staff wondered if this perfect "team" could exist.

JULIE McHENRY, high school softball coach:

It is not a college scholarship that parents should be looking for. It is the opportunity for their child to be involved in something that he loves, to set goals, and to be willing to work hard to achieve those goals. It should be about developing a well-rounded student-athlete who will learn valuable social and time management skills, the importance of a strong work ethic, and how to handle adversity and disappointment.

Coaching strategies for this highly anticipated season began as early as August 2007. Once the 2007 season was clearly over, the coaching staff began preparing for the next chapter. We felt getting the team into a fall league was key; it would identify which players were committed to the team. We had a core of five players from the 2006 and 2007 seasons who were returning, and it was great to be back together to begin a new season. Only two players decided to move on to other AAU programs.

We built the team from the core of five players. After team selection, our first order of business was to have a parents' meeting. We laid out in detail the expectations of the coaching staff for this team. We made it clear the team came first with a total team commitment and individual agendas would come second. I spoke at length about communication, trust, collective responsibility, and leadership. I stressed the adversities that inevitably would arise for each and every player at some time during the season but how this would, in the end, help foster growth and development. I discussed how playing time would not be equal, but my goal was fair playing time for each. Attendance at practice and games as well as court play would factor into playing time. My number one goal was to coach a team that bought into the system of total team play, where players were passionate about being on this Tar Heel team, with the success of the team always coming first. I wanted the players to actually care more about team goals than individual agendas. I yearned to coach, teaching all the nuances of the game, in the way I felt it should be played.

I was revived and very passionate about starting a new season. The players became aware early on that this next level of competition we were preparing them for would demand much concentration and commitment. We continued our complicated system of match-up zones and motion offenses would help prepare them for the next level of varsity high school basketball. I wanted them to learn how to think and play in the future, even in the next minute, with anticipation and not just react to what had happened in the game. I explained that this was a key skill to learn to take their game to the next level. There was also one change in the coaching hierarchy with Marc, the head coach, stepping down to assistant coach due to a career change. I now took on the role as head coach.

The new players, as expected, had trouble at first learning so much in limited practice time. I was a stickler for detail in running the offenses, and more importantly, learning every angle and movement of the match-up zone.

I was aware that if I had just thrown a ball out there and let them freelance, we would have won many more games early on, but in the end they would not have learned anything new, anything they could build on to develop into better individual players. I realized also that the learning curve takes them out of their rhythm and their game for a time, but in the end, we would become a much better team and be able to compete with the elite teams because of our system of play and our insistence for detail. I also felt that the players would come away from the season as much better individual players, and we would be preparing them well for competitive high school varsity play. We wanted to do everything in our power to make this a season to remember and develop each girl into a better all-around basketball player.

The script for the season could not have been written better. We lost our share of games early on, but we were "gelling" and learning valuable lessons as a team. We came away from each practice, each tournament, as a better team and with clear ideas as a coaching staff as to what we needed to teach and stress to make these players better. Yes, I wanted these players to work hard primarily for this team, but what actually was happening was every player was becoming a better individual player by not focusing solely on themselves. I could personally see the development of the players, and that was my goal. I wanted to be able to hand these players back to their respective high school coaches as better players in all aspects of the game of basketball. I wanted them to be true team players, something a high school coach would appreciate.

We placed third at the U-14 Mid-Atlantic Regionals and played some exceptional basketball. No, we were not the most talented individuals, but together as a team we were hard to beat. I told my players time in and time out that five less talented players playing together as one could almost always beat a team of individual players. We did not win every game, but we kept ourselves in many games by working hard as a unit. We went to Nationals in Tennessee and played well. We came away with only two wins, but we proved we belonged there.

This Tar Heel season is by far the highlight of my coaching career to this point. We were able to accomplish something so rare in this day and age. Each and every player bought into the system of five playing as one. As difficult as the prior season was only the year before, this particular season was opposite. I felt we were finally able to coach a team of individuals and have not only the girls, but also the parents, committed to the team. They rarely were thinking of themselves but had a conscious focus of being a part of the team, working hard for team goals. I ask myself many times, what was the recipe for the hundred-and-eighty-degree change in less than a year?

If I would like to try to repeat the success we had this particular season with parent and player harmony, I need to identify what went so right this season and what went so wrong in previous seasons.

- Communication with the parents from the beginning about our philosophy.

- Dealing with one disgruntled parent immediately. We as a coaching staff met with a parent and player. After having this parent/coach/player meeting, the player did stay with the team without any further animosity. We were able to talk out our differences in philosophy without bringing down the entire team.

- Being consistent with our philosophy of true team play and unselfishness. That included sitting players or pulling them out of a game if we were not happy with some of their antics, such as poor body language and individual selfish play.

- Probably the most noteworthy, coaching with the same passion and commitment we demonstrated for the past three years and not showing any negative affects of losing two players from our core group the prior year. In other words, we were now coaching the players who truly believed in us as coaches, and their parents showed respect in return. Having parents that supported the coaching staff and promoted a positive attitude allowed us to get the most out of each player. Our players played at a higher level with positive parental support.

This season was not the result of us changing our ways as coaches. Instead, it was just continuing our philosophy of beliefs in the way the game should be taught and played. For four years now, this Tar Heel coaching staff has coached with this philosophy of total team play. Even during the tough year we experienced as coaches, with parents and players not buying into this philosophy, we tried not to waver. As a result of this team's perseverance, we were given the greatest gift of all—that perfect season. I am now thankful for that difficult 2007 season in which I personally learned, developed, and grew the most as a coach. And isn't that ironic, because it is what I continue to preach to others and is, in fact, the truth. During times of adversity and struggle is when you can learn and grow the most, so never fear adversity—welcome it.

The adversity our children experience can also be the tool and the avenue to foster the most growth and development, thus facilitating them to become the best he/she can be. My lowest days as a coach in 2007 became my turning point as a coach. It also became so clear to me with the comparison of the 2007 and 2008 seasons just how much the attitude of the parent comes into play with the success not only of the team, but also the player.

DENNIS MURPHY, college athlete, parent, AAU basketball coach:

My wife and I as parents gave our children opportunities to become better. We sent them to camps, coached them in AAU and travel teams. We put up a court with lights in the backyard. But what we know now is that it is totally up to the child, the player, to want it and want it bad. They need to work hard enough to get better. They need to get fitter and stronger. I think with my coaching experience, I am much more objective of my kids' talent then most. But what I learned is that I need to know who my kid is on the court. I know that I pushed them. I wanted them to take more initiative, be more aggressive. Looking back now, and I knew it them, that was not always who my child was. "Your child is who they are." And they have personality traits and you cannot turn them into someone else. I became frustrated at the time but I see it more clearly that my child is who she is, and certain aspects cannot change. Through this process of parenting high school athletes, I have learned to pull back with each daughter. There is little preaching now with my third child. It is a little different approach. It is difficult, because the coach in us always wants to teach.

MY BIGGEST CHALLENGE: PARENTING A COLLEGE ATHLETE

I began this project feeling the pressures of being a coach and all the emotions that encompasses and suddenly I found myself buried deep in the role of being a "parent of two athletes." The difficulty and complexity of this parenting role hit me head-on with the struggles my daughter Alyssa faced playing Division III college basketball. I found myself feeling frustrated and was tested daily in trying to find the right words and support to help her through some tough times.

I realize her situation as an athlete was not unique. She initially found much success in the game she loves through the course of her first two seasons playing college ball. Then suddenly she was met with disappointment and adversity trying to deal with drastic changes in her role on the team. Alyssa was fortunate to have played in every game as a college freshman. She then became a starter as a sophomore, and although not a great scorer, she thrived as being a role player. Her junior year began, and she was named captain and had great expectations for a successful season, especially since the coaches had done such a great job recruiting and the team looked strong. Expectation can be a dangerous word, not only for a player, but also for parents. I was so excited for this season, to be a proud parent, watching my daughter play college basketball as a junior captain.

There it is—parents wanting so much for their children, wanting them to get the headlines, the glory, and the playing time. That was not what Alyssa's fate would be. But here she was at the beginning of her junior year in college and still playing basketball. I think back to all the little girls who were playing basketball when she was eight, nine, and ten years old. The number participating at her age group became fewer and fewer as she entered junior high. Then I think of all the girls that played freshman basketball and how that number was cut in half by the time they were all sophomores. By the time she was a senior in high school, there was just a small percentage still participating in the sport as senior players. This is the nature of the game, of competition. But who would have thought that at age twenty and on the doorstep to her junior year in college she would not only be still playing but would be made a captain due to her leadership qualities?

She expressed to me early on that she probably would not be a starter again this season, because the new players were talented offensively. She was preparing me and did not want me to be disappointed. I reassured her I knew things could change, but this was a great opportunity for her not to get comfortable with her game but work even harder to be the best player possible. I told her a team always needs a role player and a good defender.

Alyssa is a competitor and wants to win, first and foremost. She wants to be on a winning team and expressed to me that if her team was winning without her out on the court, then that was the right move. Since a young age, my daughters have heard me stress the team concept. I know this is why both of them think more like a coach than like a player. Out on the court, they are both unselfish to a frustrating point.

That highly anticipated junior season for Alyssa, however, became a turning point for her. Instead of having a promising season, this team had a losing record of 7-17. Alyssa was lucky to now play four minutes a game, and she felt the team was falling apart.

So there I was, with my daughter feeling so frustrated and hating what the season had become. She lost all her confidence. As a parent, it was equally frustrating for me. We, as parents, live and die with our child, as we feel helpless to make the situation better for them. Everything happens for a reason, and while I set out to write an informative book to help parents in this difficult role of "parenting an athlete," I was writing it mostly from the perspective of a coach trying to deal with difficult, disgruntled parents. I think of myself as a somewhat religious person, and I cannot help think that my daughter's struggles were a result of God giving me this worst-case scenario of dealing with a difficult situation in order to make me understand and feel every parental emotion possible.

So there was my test as a parent. What could I do to handle this situation for my daughter? But I realized this question was part of the problem. As much as I wanted to fix the situation for my daughter, I could not. I had the role of that of a parent, and I needed to support my daughter in any way possible and not place blame but help my daughter control what she could control. I needed to be her sounding board, someone she could call to vent, but I needed to try to turn it back to what she could do to make it tolerable.

I encouraged her to work on her game and try to bring it to a new level. She was barely playing at all in the games. It was obvious the focus was all about offense, shooting, and scoring. I explained to Alyssa that that was why she was playing so little. For most of her athletic career, she had been an excellent defender and a role player. In this particular season, if she was not scoring, then she was not going to play. Although I tried to stay calm and matter-of-fact, inside I was infuriated. The only thing left to do was to help her control what she could control. This was yet another opportunity for her to grow and understand through real-life issues.

Alyssa could have quit that season like many others had, but she did not want her career to end that way in the middle of a season. It was difficult, but she tried hard to find something positive to take away. She decided to work out on her own, improve her jump shot, work out in the weight room, run on her own, and by the end of the season, she was playing a little more. That was her responsibility. I told her if things had just kept rolling along in a positive manner as the previous seasons and she was playing a lot, she would not have seen the urgency to work on her game and try to become even better. She learned to not use the "role" player as a crutch to play, but found what it took to play on this team, and she worked to try to get there.

This parental role was not easy, because with each game, each loss, and each minute my daughter sat on the bench frustrated, I needed to come up with another angle to spin it to a positive. Yes, I talked about the frustrations of the season with my husband and family. Although that did make me feel better for the moment, it did nothing to remedy the situation and improve it for my child. I knew if I had started pointing fingers or bad-mouthed the coach to other parents and, worse yet, to my daughter, it would have done nothing to make the situation better except possibly make me feel better for a moment. I knew it was not about me. It was about doing something in my power to help my daughter.

The bottom line that I learn time and time again is to try to spin every adversity into a positive. This was the most challenging situation for me, because there was little to say to my frustrated daughter. But I made Alyssa, and myself too, realize again that sports are a direct correlation with life's lessons. This did not seem like a fair situation, but life is not fair either. We have two choices: complain and blame others when things do not go our way, or work hard to make it better even if it appears to be an impossible situation. The next move was to stop complaining (me included) and try to become a better person foremost and a better player because of the experience. I am proud to say her leadership, character, and integrity screamed out that entire season. She cheered on everyone from the bench. I know this was not an easy task, but she made a conscience effort to still be that captain, that leader.

Years from now we will not remember this season with such negative emotion. If it had been a fairy tale season for her, I would have been so happy and proud. But how long would I remember that, and how much would she have grown as a person and a player? I will look back years from now and remember all the adversity and all the moments that challenged her integrity, character, and leadership, and I *will* remember this season as a great learning experience in her life, and I may even thank God for putting her in this situation to prepare her for the trials and tribulations that lie ahead for her.

Personally, I did not come out of this season proud of the way I handled this adversity as a parent. Yes, I am proud of my daughter and how she handled the situation, but I lost so much sleep churning, frustrated, feeling everything parents feel. If we can give negative situations a positive spin, it is a gift to our children in the long journey of life. This is challenging because as parents, we are not programmed to sit idly by and not make a statement. We must allow our children to experience all that life has to offer and hopefully grow with the positive, as well as the negative, experiences.

I personally understand what a parent goes through raising an athlete. It is so difficult, encompassing every human emotion. Through my experiences of parenting an athlete, I have learned so much on my journey and want to share this lesson. Sometimes as parents, we just need to sit back and watch our children live life and all that that entails. We must learn how to spin adversity into something positive. That sometimes is the best way we can help our children grow when faced with difficult situations.

DENNIS MURPHY:

The advice that I would tell parents is to relax, keep everything in perspective. The parent watching the child competing needs to enjoy the game. Parents need to keep the sports situation in perspective. In the end, the child, not the parent, has to want it for himself. I wanted my children to be as good as they could be. I knew they could be better than they showed at times. But the child has to work hard for that. The child, not the parent, has to have the passion for the game.

DR. JIM KARUSTIS,
FAMILY PSYCHOLOGIST

The pressures exerted upon children by their parents are largely unintentional. It is socially unacceptable, for example, for a parent to scream at a child on the soccer field, "Come on! You can do better than that! Score, score, score!"—or some such. Though that, of course, does not stop any number of parents from acting this way. One parent with whom I have worked in therapy related a traumatic experience. He was filling in as an assistant for his son's middle school basketball team, and the head coach (Coach X) on the other team was also a parent. He was hostile, negativistic, and belligerent, and made explicit statements to his players throughout the game, with the message that unless they were bleeding, slipping in their own sweat, and gagging from thirst that they were clearly not trying sufficiently hard to win. He was a forbidding character, and though there was mumbling among players and on-lookers (including his own son on the team), no one said a word to him. I learned this was typical of the way this coach was handled. When my patient finally confronted Coach X about his overly physically aggressive manner, Coach X erupted. My client wanted to "do the right thing" and to model decent, mature problem solving for his child. This situation only avoided physical violence by my client getting in his car and driving away.

I bring this scenario up because of the focus I wish to place on the parents in the audience. Experience has taught me that fear, being cowed by such a character as Coach X, is only part of the explanation for their lack of responsibility. In private, parents will tell me how much they envy physically aggressive competition. Those who are against such an approach generally take a "What are you going to do?" attitude and do nothing or, more insidiously, quietly remove their children from competitive sports. So over time we see imbalance and those remaining either not enjoying the process or implicitly joining the camp of Coach X.

The indirect, and hence more pervasive, unconscious, and longer-lasting effects come in from parental fears and anxieties. There is much talk in families of "living up to one's potential." Sounds good, but what does it mean? Again, the question of balance. The message is either children must become so focused on competitive sports that other aspects of life suffer or they are slackers. With the images of drug taking, sexually active kids and teens in the back of parents' minds, these seem like the only two choices. As a psychologist, I see children already have so few role models for what could be "normal" life that if the parents do not model balance, along with integration of values with daily life, youngsters will almost certainly *not* get it elsewhere.

In the therapy room, it is one of the most difficult issues to address, because parents are so rarely aware of their own attitudes and beliefs. Fathers are so often criticized for "fear of intimacy," but mothers are so often just as guilty of this criticism. My point is that when kids are overly encouraged, indeed pushed, into hyper-activity or, as some say, "over-scheduling" with sports, this action is reinforced by many in society, including schools and friends and extended family members. The child will be praised, certainly. Over time, there is less and less time for parents and kids to just be together, with no "have to" items on the schedule. And hence the critical points in which parents and kids should be getting closer, getting to *know* one another, are missed. Reflection, retreat, processing of experiences does not have a chance to be nurtured.

JULIE McHENRY, parent, high school softball coach:

Parents have taken a very active role in the development of their athletes. They have invested many hours, many dollars, and sacrificed many weekends in the pursuit of excellence for their child. They have coached their daughters' teams, practiced with them in their backyards, paid for private instruction, morphed tournaments in Florida and California into family vacations. They have developed their daughters into better softball players, but have also developed an attitude of entitlement. They believed their child was the best, worked the hardest, and deserved to be a varsity starter, or the star, or the shortstop, or the number three hitter in the lineup because of the work they put in. I think parents sometimes lose their objectivity when assessing their daughters' talent, because of the time and monetary investments they themselves have made.

"WHERE IS MY TROPHY?"

We, as parents, have to ask ourselves many important questions throughout the "parenting an athlete" journey—questions we as individual parents can only answer for ourselves. The answers are unique and personal for each parent. It is our deepest thoughts and feeling in how we raise our own children.

So at the end of my day, in this final chapter of my life parenting a high school and college athlete, I ask myself, why do I want my children to compete in sports? Is my main focus that they are the stars of every team they play on? Am I looking for them to gain recognition and be the envy of the school? Do I yearn to be that proud parent sitting in the stands saying, "That's my kid"? Or is it just good enough for my child to be challenged and step up … possibly be a leader? Am I missing the opportunities that allow them to blossom to become what they can ultimately be? We, as humans, are so programmed for immediate results, gratification, and rewards. We do not allow any time in our day for just so-so. We teach our children to be the best and to work hard for that coveted prize that is right there at their fingertips.

But what if there is no immediate prize? What if there is just the satisfaction of a job done, and maybe even not "that well done?" What if not being the best is still okay? I am a competitor and a perfectionist, and I see the opportunities in everything. I too want my children to excel, but I do not want them to think that because they do something ordinary they are entitled to immediate gratification, a prize.

My generation of parents right now has attempted to make everything "fair." At times we want to shield our children from the pressure of competing and the disappointment of not being the best, so we believe everyone should be rewarded for just "showing up." This is sending the wrong message to our children in that "If they do this, then they will get that." Life is not like that, and everything is not always perfect and fair. Opportunities are a gift, and rewards should never be expected.

What I am saying and what is a strange concept for me to understand is what has now become the normal practice on many teams today. That is presenting every child on every team with a trophy just for participating in that sport. The prize for being on a team should be the privilege of being a member of that team. Trophies are given out so routinely today that the significance is diluted.

My daughter Kristina has so many trophies around the house that she rarely looks at them and I know has little appreciation for them. I mentioned earlier about my first trophy earned after winning a CYO championship. I placed my trophy in its own little shrine. I glanced at it almost every day, reliving the relevance to what that trophy actually represented. It was special to me because not everyone received one, and it was truly an award.

If we continue to allow our children to expect awards for just doing the minimal, will they understand what it will take to go above and beyond? Four short words sum up what has lifted most successful individuals above the crowd: "A little bit more." They did what was expected and ... a little bit more.

Are we setting our children up for disappointment later on in high school when they need to compete for a place on the team where not everyone makes the team and not everyone gets equal playing time? Are they going to quit because they feel such disappointment? Do they have the attitude of entitlement because so early on in life they were programmed that everyone "got a trophy"?

The opportunities available for children to grow and develop, to experience the thrills of success and the difficulties with defeat, sure outweigh any plastic trophy given for just being on a team. We need to reinforce this concept to our children and ourselves about the dangers in expectations. They need to know our only expectation is that they try their best, which in no way means they are the best. Then if at the end of the day they win a trophy, they should relish it, because it was something earned, and it was unique, not handed out to everyone. Each award, each trophy earned should have a story, a memory behind it that grows more precious and special with each passing year.

I have a responsibility to myself on my journey, as a parent and most importantly to my child, to do the best job possible in raising an athlete. I recognize the enormous importance of this parenting role in the development of the child. Sadly, I realize I am in the home stretch of watching my own children compete in the high school and college arena. As a parent, I do not get to do it all over again. This is not practice; this is life. I hope I have appreciated every minute watching my daughters go from little girls, having fun playing the game, to becoming serious athletes. Hopefully I have supported them unconditionally, not only with their successes but also, more importantly, during the times of intense pressure of competing. We must be prepared not only for all of their success, but the disappointments that do go hand in hand.

Being a parent of an athlete means being our child's rock, our child's supporter, no matter what. Ultimately, that becomes "our" trophy. In the end, will we have great memories in our heart with no regrets? Will we be able to look back and say I would not have done anything differently? Will our children look back at us with heartfelt appreciation for our unwavering support no matter how they played, even if they were not the best or they did not win? Will we be proud of all of our words and actions to our children, the officials, the coaches, to other players and parents? Will we know deep down we did not push them to the breaking point, but truly helped them along their journey … not ours?

And finally, ask yourself, how will I feel ten years from now? What really will matter for me and for my child—athletics? What effect long range, both physically and emotionally, did I have on my child? And lastly, how well did I play the game … the game of "Parenting an Athlete?" Would I have won a trophy?